# FINDING PEACE

*Letting Go of Stress and Worry*

Amy Ekeh

## Little Rock
### Scripture Study

*A ministry of the Diocese of Little Rock*
*in partnership with Liturgical Press*

*Nihil obstat:* Jerome Kodell, OSB, *Censor Librorum.*
*Imprimatur:* ✠ Anthony B. Taylor, Bishop of Little Rock, November 27, 2018.

Cover design by Ann Blattner. Cover photo: Getty Images. Used with permission.

Photos/illustrations: Pages 7, 10, 14, 17, 21, 25, 28, 29, 34, 36, 39, Getty Images. Used with permission.

ISBN: 978-0-8146-6402-5 (print); 978-0-8146-6426-1 (ebook)

# Contents

# Introduction

**Alive in the Word** brings you resources to deepen your understanding of Scripture, offer meaning for your life today, and help you to pray and act in response to God's word.

Use any volume of **Alive in the Word** in the way best suited to you.

- **For individual learning and reflection,** consider this an invitation to prayerfully journal in response to the questions you find along the way. And be prepared to move from head to heart and then to action.

- **For group learning and reflection,** arrange for three sessions where you will use the material provided as the basis for faith sharing and prayer. You may ask group members to read each chapter in advance and come prepared with questions answered. In this kind of session, plan to be together for about an hour. Or, if your group prefers, read and respond to the questions together without advance preparation. With this approach, it's helpful to plan on spending more time for each group session in order to adequately work through each of the chapters.

- **For a parish-wide event or use within a larger group,** provide each person with a copy of this volume, and allow time during the event for quiet reading, group discussion and prayer, and then a final commitment by each person to some simple action in response to what he or she learned.

This volume on the topic of finding peace is one of several volumes that explore **Seasons of Our Lives.** While the Scriptures remain constant, we have the opportunity to find within them a fresh message as we go through life facing various challenges. Whether the circumstances in our lives change due to our own decisions or due to the natural process of aging and maturing, we bring with us the actual lived experiences of this world to our prayerful reading of the Bible. This series provides an opportunity to acknowledge our own circumstances and to find how God continues to work in us through changing times.

# Prologue

There are no easy solutions when it comes to stress. Modern life is an often-perplexing blend of things to do, decisions to make, and lists to remember. In the midst of it all, we face the daily challenges of health, relationships, and finances. From small problems to large, it is easy to feel overwhelmed, worried, and on edge.

Many things can help us cope with worry and stress, including lifestyle changes and finding ways to decrease the pressure we so often place on ourselves. Our faith also plays a key role in restoring peace in our lives. Of course, reading Scripture prayerfully—as we will do together in this book—does not "fix" stress or eliminate worry. But it can help us on our quest for peace. Scripture repeatedly reminds us of God's abiding love for us and his desire that we find peace—and indeed joy—in our lives. This does not mean that we will never suffer or struggle, but it does mean that we have a Shepherd who carries us close to his heart.

Together we will read and reflect on three Scripture passages that will take us on a journey into peace. First, Jesus will assure us of God's loving care and will challenge us to trust in it. Second, we will reflect on how our struggles unite us more closely with the death—and the life—of Christ. And finally, we will come to the triumphant conclusion that it is in love for others that we find the greatest peace of all.

# Do Not Be Afraid

*Begin by quietly asking God to assist you in your prayer and study. Then read the passage from Luke 12 where Jesus encourages his followers not to worry.*

## Luke 12:22-34

²²[Jesus] said to [his] disciples, "Therefore I tell you, do not worry about your life and what you will eat, or about your body and what you will wear. ²³For life is more than food and the body more than clothing. ²⁴Notice the ravens: they do not sow or reap; they have neither storehouse nor barn, yet God feeds them. How much more important are you than birds! ²⁵Can any of you by worrying add a moment to your lifespan? ²⁶If even the smallest things are beyond your control, why are you anxious about the rest? ²⁷Notice how the flowers grow. They do not toil or spin. But I tell you, not even Solomon in all his splendor was dressed like one of them. ²⁸If God so clothes the grass in the field that grows today and is thrown

into the oven tomorrow, will he not much more provide for you, O you of little faith? 29As for you, do not seek what you are to eat and what you are to drink, and do not worry anymore. 30All the nations of the world seek for these things, and your Father knows that you need them. 31Instead, seek his kingdom, and these other things will be given you besides. 32Do not be afraid any longer, little flock, for your Father is pleased to give you the kingdom.33Sell your belongings and give alms. Provide money bags for yourselves that do not wear out, an inexhaustible treasure in heaven that no thief can reach nor moth destroy. 34For where your treasure is, there also will your heart be."

*Following a few moments of quiet reflection on the passage from the Gospel of Luke, consider the information provided in Setting the Scene. The occasional questions in the margins may be used for personal reflection or for group discussion.*

## Setting the Scene

**What do you worry about? What are some of the sources of stress in your life?**

Few Scripture passages are as comforting—or as challenging—as this excerpt from Luke's gospel, sometimes called the "discourse on worry." It comforts us as it declares God's loving care for us, and it challenges us to the very core of our being, urging us to reprioritize our lives by trusting wholeheartedly in God.

As we explore this discourse on worry, it may be helpful to reflect on the broader context and to consider Jesus' own state of mind as he speaks these words. This discourse is situated squarely in what is known as Luke's "travel narrative" (9:51–19:27). In this lengthy section of the gospel, Jesus has "resolutely determined" (9:51) to journey to Jerusalem despite the suffering that awaits him there (9:22). Along the way, Jesus preaches to large crowds and to his disciples, teaching them everything they need to know to be his disciples.

In a sense, Jesus is preparing his followers for his own death and resurrection, which will be a turning point in salvation history. Jesus is obviously resolved to face whatever awaits him in Jerusalem, yet there is genuine anxiety involved in facing death (as we clearly see in Jesus' agony in the Garden of Gethsemane in Luke 22:39-46). Indeed, as we hear Jesus encouraging us to let go of worry and refocus our minds and hearts on God's unfailing love, we are hearing the words of a man who is facing this enormous spiritual endeavor himself.

The immediate context of the discourse on worry is also important. As Jesus preaches to the crowds, a man calls out to him: "Teacher, tell my brother to share the inheritance with me!" (12:13). Jesus has no interest in this family disagreement, but he takes the opportunity to teach about greed. He proceeds to tell the parable of the rich fool (12:16-21), a short story about a man whose land yields a remarkable harvest. Satisfied and even a bit giddy, the man makes plans to build newer, larger barns to hold the bounty. But before he can do so, he abruptly dies,

and God calls him a fool. Obsessed with himself and his own plans (his dialogue is excessively peppered with the words "I" and "my"), this man has attained earthly success but has tragically failed to secure lasting joy, happiness, or peace.

Jesus' discourse on worry expands upon this story. Focusing on ourselves—our crops, barns, and wealth, our own plans and personal notions of success—will not bring us peace. Only a radical trust in a loving God can do that.

*Luke 12:22-34 will be explored a few verses at a time to deepen your understanding and appreciation.*

### Understanding the Scene Itself

²²He said to [his] disciples, "Therefore I tell you, do not worry about your life and what you will eat, or about your body and what you will wear. ²³For life is more than food and the body more than clothing.

When reflecting upon the words of Jesus in the gospels, it is always helpful to notice who he is addressing. For example, Jesus tends to speak quite differently to the Pharisees than to a weeping sinner or a desperate parent.

In this discourse, Luke tells us that Jesus is speaking "to his disciples." This is noteworthy for several reasons. First, Jesus is not known for "going easy" on his closest followers. He sometimes seems to tire of explaining things to them (Mark 4:13) as he pushes them to understand and accept difficult, challenging teachings (Luke 9:22-23). And yet it is obvious that Jesus loves his disciples deeply. He shares with them intimate truths about God's kingdom (Mark 4:11). He keeps them close to him in his darkest hour (Matt 26:37). He calls them "friends" (John 15:15). Here, in this discourse, Jesus is both demanding and loving. This is the stance of a master teacher with his disciples.

The fact that Jesus is speaking to his disciples is important for another reason: we too are Jesus' disciples. When we read this text, we know that Jesus is speaking to *us*—just as immediately and intimately as he spoke to them. He will not "go easy" on us, but we do not really want him to. We want him to place the same demands on us that he placed on his first disciples. And we know that along with those demands comes his deep and abiding love. Just as they did for Jesus' original followers, these words will help us to become better disciples.

Jesus begins his discourse with a simple directive: "do not worry." As quickly as these words

Have you had any teachers, family members, or mentors who held you to a very high standard because they cared about you? How did their expectations and encouragement help to shape you?

bring us solace, they may also create questions and even frustration in our minds: *How are we to follow this advice? How do we stop worrying? What do we do with our anxiety?* As we read on, we will find that Jesus is indeed offering us solace, but he does so by calling us to completely reassess our priorities. Instead of adopting the priorities of the world—the obvious preoccupations like our finances, our work, our future, our appearance, and our health ("your life and what you will eat . . . your body and what you will wear")—Jesus is calling us to adopt the even more fulfilling priorities of discipleship ("life is *more* than food and the body *more* than clothing").

**²⁴Notice the ravens: they do not sow or reap; they have neither storehouse nor barn, yet God feeds them. How much more important are you than birds!**

Jesus elaborates on his "do not worry" maxim by offering his disciples an engaging example from nature. The raven does not live as though it is concerned about the future. It does not plant or store food in order to have enough. The raven simply lives day by day, relying completely on nature's bounty.

Jesus' reference to "storehouses" and "barns" may remind us of the parable of the rich fool that immediately precedes this discourse. The rich man exclaimed that he would build newer, bigger barns to store all of his success, and in doing so he became dependent not upon God, but solely upon himself. This is not the carefree, trusting life of the raven.

One more note about this verse. Ravens were considered unclean by Jews (Deut 14:14). In telling this story, Jesus does not choose the most beautiful or graceful bird for us to emulate. Rather, he chooses a common scavenger bird. And then he tells us that "God feeds them." In other words, we do not have to be a certain kind of person before God will take care of us. God will care for every single thing that he created, and that includes each one of us. No exceptions.

> How can we strike a balance between sensibly planning for the future and excessively worrying about it?

<sup>25</sup>**Can any of you by worrying add a moment to your lifespan? <sup>26</sup>If even the smallest things are beyond your control, why are you anxious about the rest? <sup>27</sup>Notice how the flowers grow. They do not toil or spin. But I tell you, not even Solomon in all his splendor was dressed like one of them. <sup>28</sup>If God so clothes the grass in the field that grows today and is thrown into the oven tomorrow, will he not much more provide for you, O you of little faith?**

As Jesus continues, two rhetorical questions offer some basic common sense and help us rethink the energy we expend on worrying about the future: *Can worrying about the future add a moment to your life? Haven't you noticed that*

What is the best advice anyone ever gave you about dealing with worry or anxiety? How have you implemented it into your life?

*nothing is ever fully under your control?* Reflection on this candid philosophy may save us a great deal of "fretting" over things we cannot control.

Like the example of the ravens, Jesus shares another example from nature: flowers. Some translations are more specific, identifying the flowers as "lilies" (NRSV). Known for their beauty (even more beautiful than a wealthy king's wardrobe!), lilies are also ephemeral, short-lived, like the grass that grows one day and is burned for fuel the next. Is something that lives such a short time worth God's care? All we need to do is look upon a lily to answer in the affirmative. Jesus' conclusion is not far behind: If God makes something that lives such a short time beautiful, won't he care for you who are so valuable? Won't God make your life beautiful too?

Jesus' description of his disciples being of "little faith" actually serves as further encouragement. Our faith may be small at times—too small to place our full trust in God, too small to

14   *Finding Peace, Letting Go of Stress and Worry*

hand our futures over to God, too small to completely reset our priorities as disciples—and yet our faith *does* exist. It can always grow—like a mustard seed (Luke 13:19) or a pinch of yeast (Luke 13:21)—into something much greater.

**²⁹As for you, do not seek what you are to eat and what you are to drink, and do not worry anymore. ³⁰All the nations of the world seek for these things, and your Father knows that you need them. ³¹Instead, seek his kingdom, and these other things will be given you besides. ³²Do not be afraid any longer, little flock, for your Father is pleased to give you the kingdom.**

Verse 29 is almost incomprehensible when read by itself. Jesus is advising his disciples against two very typical human behaviors: focusing on food and drink (i.e., physical survival) and worrying. How could we possibly stop doing either of these things? Verse 30 sheds light on this question. First, Jesus points out that the "nations of the world" (or the Gentiles, those who are not in relationship with God) are focused on material things, implying that those who know God should know better. Second, Jesus tells us that the reason we do not need to worry is because *God already knows we need these things.* And if God already knows, we can rest assured that he will provide for us what we need, much as he cares for the ravens and the lilies.

Because God already knows our needs and will provide for us, we can focus our time and energy on other things. Jesus urges us to focus

The Greek verb that is translated as "worry" in verse 29 is *meteorizō*, which literally means "to hang in the air." What does worrying feel like to you? Why is it so destructive?

Jesus says that God will provide for our needs. But there are many people in this world who do not have what they need. How might we pray and think about this? Do we have a role to play?

The message "do not be afraid" or "do not fear" is a common refrain in Scripture (e.g., Gen 15:1; Acts 18:9). Why do you think God repeats these words to us so many times?

on the kingdom of God. The kingdom of God is the healing, saving, transforming presence of God in the world, especially present in the ministry and person of Jesus. This focus on the kingdom of God is what discipleship is all about. It requires an enormous amount of trust and surrender, a total shift in perspective, an intimate relationship with God. This intimate relationship with God is ultimately what allows us to follow Jesus' advice—to stop worrying (v. 29), to not be afraid (v. 32). According to Jesus, those who know God are as free as the birds.

Jesus' reference to his disciples as "little flock" is a comforting detail. In Jesus' time, his audience may have heard beautiful echoes of the prophet Ezekiel ("I myself will pasture my sheep; I myself will give them rest. . . . The lost I will search out, the strays I will bring back, the injured I will bind up, and the sick I will heal"; 34:15-16) or the psalms ("The LORD is my shepherd; / there is nothing I lack. / In green pastures he makes me lie down; / to still waters he leads me; / he restores my soul"; 23:1-2). The refrain echoes once again: *God loves us; he will care for us.*

> [33]Sell your belongings and give alms. Provide money bags for yourselves that do not wear out, an inexhaustible treasure in heaven that no thief can reach nor moth destroy. [34]For where your treasure is, there also will your heart be."

The final words of Jesus' discourse urge the disciples one step further. Not only should they not *worry* about what they will eat, drink, and wear, but they should actually sell what they *do* have and give to the poor! What Jesus asks is difficult, but it is meant to bring total freedom and absolute peace. The more we clutter our lives with things, with complications, with burdens, the more stressed and anxious we become. But

when we are able to hear and understand the words of Jesus, when we let go of unnecessary attachments, release our burdens, and restore our hearts in God's love, then we will be free.

A final note of realism emerges in these last verses of the discourse on worry. Jesus' reference to "inexhaustible treasure in heaven" that cannot be destroyed by the ups and downs of human life reminds us that for now, loss and pain are part of our earthly reality. Jesus himself will walk on to Jerusalem, where he will be verbally assaulted, physically tortured, and violently killed. Clearly, trust in God's care and providence does not mean that bad things will never happen to us. It does not mean that we will never go without or that we will never be in pain. But the radical dependence on God that Jesus encourages us to embrace means that *we will always be with the God whose kingdom, whose love, already surrounds us*. Like Jesus himself, no matter what we experience, no matter what we lose, our treasure is in that which

How do you reconcile the belief that God will care for us with the reality that bad things still happen to us? How can the example of Jesus' death (and resurrection) help us understand this?

can never be stolen or destroyed—God's inexhaustible love for us.

## Praying the Word / Sacred Reading

*Stress was clearly an issue in Jesus' day just as it is in ours. In the passage below, Jesus encourages one of his friends to let go of her anxiety and worry. Ponder the story. Then say the prayer provided, or offer a heartfelt prayer of your own.*

> As they continued their journey he entered a village where a woman whose name was Martha welcomed him. She had a sister named Mary [who] sat beside the Lord at his feet listening to him speak. Martha, burdened with much serving, came to him and said, "Lord, do you not care that my sister has left me by myself to do the serving? Tell her to help me." The Lord said to her in reply, "Martha, Martha, you are anxious and worried about many things. There is need of only one thing. Mary has chosen the better part and it will not be taken from her." (Luke 10:38-42)

Lord Jesus, your friends Martha and Mary both loved you. Martha wanted to express her love by serving, and perhaps at times she did so with joy. But on this day, she was burdened, anxious, and worried.

Mary sat with you, listening, at peace. This was "the better part"—to focus on you, your voice, and your words. This was the "one thing" that was needed that day.

Gently teach me, Lord, to sit, to listen, to let go of my burdens, to set aside the many things that make me anxious and worried. May I too find peace listening to your voice, focused on you as you speak into my heart: "Do not be afraid."

## Living the Word

*The beginnings of worry are not necessarily destructive. Sometimes worry and stress can motivate us to make a needed change or are natural expressions of our concern and affection for loved ones. But when worry gains momentum and cripples us, it can be spiritually and even physically draining.*

*This week, try to make a conscious effort to identify any worries you have and intentionally respond to each one with a simple action or a prayer of trust.*

*Examples of taking action in response to stress:*

- *Reach out to someone you have been worried about.*

- *Spend time with a friend or loved one.*

- *Have that difficult talk with your boss, spouse, or friend, and clear the air.*

- *Help someone who needs you in a concrete way.*

- *Apologize or accept an apology.*

- *Change your lifestyle in some small way to benefit your health.*

*Examples of prayers in response to stress:*

- *"I can't. You must. I'm yours. Show me the way." (St. Óscar Romero)*

- *"God, grant me the serenity to accept the things I cannot change, courage to change the things I can, and wisdom to know the difference." (Serenity Prayer)*

*At times, we may need help processing our anxieties so we can restore peace in our lives. If you feel that your worry, stress, or anxiety is interfering with your daily life and happiness, resolve to seek help with a counselor or mental health professional who can help you process deeply rooted anxiety or debilitating patterns of stress and worry.*

# Renewed Day by Day

*Begin in quiet, asking God to assist you in your prayer and study. Then read the passage from the Second Letter to the Corinthians, as Paul speaks words of encouragement in the midst of affliction.*

## 2 Corinthians 4:7-18

[7]But we hold this treasure in earthen vessels, that the surpassing power may be of God and not from us. [8]We are afflicted in every way, but not constrained; perplexed, but not driven to despair; [9]persecuted, but not abandoned; struck down, but not destroyed; [10]always carrying about in the body the dying of Jesus, so that the life of Jesus may also be manifested in our body. [11]For we who live are constantly being given up to death for the sake of Jesus, so that the life of Jesus may be manifested in our mortal flesh.

¹²So death is at work in us, but life in you. ¹³Since, then, we have the same spirit of faith, according to what is written, "I believed, therefore I spoke," we too believe and therefore speak, ¹⁴knowing that the one who raised the Lord Jesus will raise us also with Jesus and place us with you in his presence. ¹⁵Everything indeed is for you, so that the grace bestowed in abundance on more and more people may cause the thanksgiving to overflow for the glory of God.

¹⁶Therefore, we are not discouraged; rather, although our outer self is wasting away, our inner self is being renewed day by day. ¹⁷For this momentary light affliction is producing for us an eternal weight of glory beyond all comparison, ¹⁸as we look not to what is seen but to what is unseen; for what is seen is transitory, but what is unseen is eternal.

*Following a few moments of quiet reflection on the passage from Paul to the Corinthians, consider the information provided in Setting the Scene. Use the occasional questions in the margins for personal reflection or for group discussion.*

### Setting the Scene

In our first passage, Jesus taught his disciples about the value of trusting rather than worrying. We may find this advice theoretically meaningful but difficult to put into practice. It is not easy to simply stop worrying. As we turn to an excerpt from 2 Corinthians, we will engage with a very different kind of text. While Paul will continue urging us toward faith and trust, he does so while frankly acknowledging the aches, pains, and struggles of life. But in acknowledging them, he does not wallow in them. On the contrary, in typical Pauline fashion, he perceives in any human struggle a tremendous triumph—that of the life, death, and resurrection of Jesus Christ.

Paul is known for a profound theology that relates all pain to the transforming cross of Christ. No struggle is without meaning, no pain without purpose, no loss without gain. Vowing to "know nothing . . . except Jesus Christ, and him crucified" (1 Cor 2:2), Paul understands and teaches that life is a grand paradox—nothing is as it seems to be. Indeed, it is always much, much more.

The key to Paul's theology is this: those who believe in Christ are so closely joined with him that they are actually "in Christ" (e.g., Rom 8:1; 2 Cor 5:17). Paul even speaks of himself this way: "[I]t is no longer I who live, but it is Christ who lives in me" (Gal 2:20, NRSV). When we are "in Christ" we share in his life. Of course, this means that we also share in his death. And this is precisely what Jesus has asked us to do: "Whoever wishes to come after me must . . . take up his cross" (Mark 8:34), and "No disciple is above his teacher" (Matt 10:24).

Why do you think Jesus wants us to share in his cross? Does sharing in Jesus' cross tend to increase or decrease your stress? Does it increase or decrease your sense of peace?

In this brief but powerful excerpt from Paul's second letter to the Christian community in Corinth, new light will shine on our quest for peace. Life is much more than meets the eye. Pain, even death, will not have the final word. In Christ we are renewed, refreshed, sustained, and even brought to glory. It turns out that Jesus was right—there is no need to worry; there is nothing to fear.

Before we begin, a bit of historical context may be helpful. As modern readers we take Paul's authority for granted, but at the time of his apostolic ministry, Paul was constantly challenged by rival preachers. Paul's "brand" of the Gospel (the Good News about the life, death, and resurrection of Jesus) was novel and daring, and it was often opposed by more traditional voices. Paul also experienced the challenge of being a traveling missionary. Once he established a community in a particular region and was confident that it was strong in faith and leadership, Paul moved on to preach elsewhere. This sometimes created a situation in which other missionaries came into his fledgling communities and challenged his authority and his Gospel.

Such was the case with the young Christian community in Corinth. As a result of this pastoral crisis in which apparent factions supporting different missionaries were arising within the Corinthian community, Paul spills a great deal of ink defending the legitimacy, and even the superiority, of his own apostleship. He does so out of love and affection, not arrogance. Paul wants his people to know that his apostleship is legitimate because the content of his preaching is so essential for their understanding of their own transformation in Christ.

*2 Corinthians 4:7-18 will be explored a few verses at a time to deepen your understanding and appreciation.*

## Understanding the Scene Itself

**⁷But we hold this treasure in earthen vessels, that the surpassing power may be of God and not from us.**

In this excerpt from 2 Corinthians, Paul is writing about his ministry. The "treasure" that he writes about is his Gospel, the truth about Jesus Christ and the transforming power of his death and resurrection. Paul wants the Corinthians to know that he has suffered for the sake of this Gospel—but that his suffering is nothing short of a declaration of faith in Christ and a sign of his love for the Corinthians themselves.

Paul describes carrying this Gospel, this truth, in "earthen vessels" (or "clay jars"; NRSV). This is a humble self-description! Paul is the fragile, simple, easily chipped, limited, very human "vessel" in which the truth about Jesus Christ is kept and then shared. Paul explains that this is as it should be. There is no strength in Paul himself; the power of the Gospel is God's alone.

You may notice that in this passage Paul uses "we" instead of "I." Paul had multiple coworkers who were an essential part of his ministry. It is likely that in this passage, he is speaking of himself as part of a ministry "team" rather than just a solo missionary.

⁸We are afflicted in every way, but not constrained; perplexed, but not driven to despair; ⁹persecuted, but not abandoned; struck down, but not destroyed; ¹⁰always carrying about in the body the dying of Jesus, so that the life of Jesus may also be manifested in our body. ¹¹For we who live are constantly being given up to death for the sake of Jesus, so that the life of Jesus may be manifested in our mortal flesh.

¹²So death is at work in us, but life in you.

As the description of Paul's ministry continues, four antitheses (opposites) speak to his experience as an apostle of Jesus Christ. In each case, a negative experience is described in such a way that the negativity never overwhelms Paul. He is afflicted, perplexed, persecuted, and struck down—but he is *not* constrained ("crushed"; NRSV), driven to despair, abandoned, or destroyed. How reassuring these words are! Like Paul, we too are fragile "clay jars" who will experience trials and tribulations—we too will feel "struck down" at times. But because we do not depend on our own power but on the power of God working through us, we will never be crushed or destroyed.

A fascinating phrase elaborates on Paul's description of the trials of his ministry: "always carrying about in the body the dying of Jesus." The Greek word that is translated as "dying" is *nekrōsis*, a term used in the medical field to describe decaying tissue. Continuing in the spirit of opposites, Paul counteracts this graphic image of death; it is through this painful process of

What antithesis (set of opposites) could you use to describe your own life, as Paul does in verses 8-9?

dying with Christ that the "life of Jesus" is made manifest in Paul.

It is difficult to wrap our minds around the depths of this declaration. This is the very heart of Paul's christological outlook (his understanding of Christ). It is the underpinning of his entire life and ministry. Suffering exists, but it has no power of its own. Rather, it is a privileged sharing in the passion, the dying, of Jesus, which exists to transform, to bring life!

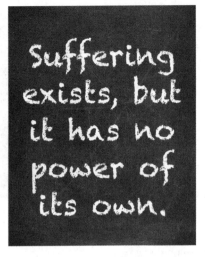

In verse 11, Paul essentially repeats this pairing of death and life, emphasizing that it is "we who live" who experience this. In other words, it happens *now*. We do not wait for death to die with Jesus or to live with him. We are already dying with him, and we already have some share in his abundant life.

Verse 12 is a testament to the selflessness of Paul's ministry. In the persecution and affliction Paul experiences (vv. 8-9), he willingly "dies" so that others may have "life." Or, more accurately, he dies *with Christ* so that others may share in the life *of Christ*. By pouring the Gospel out of the "earthen vessel" of his own body, Paul, like Christ, is laying down his life for others.

The perspective shared in this section of Paul's letter has great potential in shaping our own outlook on life and its inevitable challenges. Like Paul, we will experience low times—very low times—but without despair, without being

In 1 Corinthians 15:31, Paul writes, "I die every day!" (NRSV). What do you think Paul means by this? In what ways do you experience this?

What are some ways that you share in the life of Jesus even when going through difficult times?

crushed, without being abandoned, without being destroyed. The "deaths" or losses we experience are not empty experiences. They are, truthfully, sharings in the dying of Jesus who willingly gave himself for us—a dying that brings life. This is the Pauline paradox to lay hold of: we believe that life can be at work in us right along with death. In Christ, the two seemingly opposed experiences are inextricably interwoven.

[13]Since, then, we have the same spirit of faith, according to what is written, "I believed, therefore I spoke," we too believe and therefore speak, [14]knowing that the one who raised the Lord Jesus will raise us also with Jesus and place us with you in his presence. [15]Everything indeed is for you, so that the grace bestowed in abundance on more and more people may cause the thanksgiving to overflow for the glory of God.

Paul continues to write about his own ministry in relation to the people he serves. He quotes Psalm 116, a prayer that declares firm faith in God who saves us from death and affliction: "I believed, therefore I spoke [up]" (116:10). It is this firm faith in the midst of struggle that gives Paul the confidence to say that he knows "that the one who raised the Lord Jesus will raise us also with Jesus." In the previous section (vv. 8-12), Paul was writing about our participation in the life of Jesus in the present. But here his focus seems to shift to the future, to the Parousia (the second coming of Christ) at the end of time. When that time comes, the God who raised Jesus will raise us also and place us together in his presence.

Here, Paul introduces a new element of hope to the one who suffers, a new way of understanding the limits of human difficulty: *suffering is temporary*. Although we find profound meaning in our suffering because it gives us a share in the death and life of Jesus, we can also look forward to a time when suffering will be no more, when we will be placed in the presence of the one who raises Jesus (and us) from the dead.

Psalm 116 (like many other psalms) is a declaration of faith in God during a time of trial. Do trials shake or strengthen your faith? How might declaring our faith in God at such times help us?

Verse 15 is classically Pauline. "Everything"— Paul's Gospel, his ministry, his suffering—is "for you," for the Corinthians, for his churches. But why? So that "grace" and "thanksgiving" (*eucharistia* in Greek) may flow in abundance, giving all the glory to God.

[16]Therefore, we are not discouraged; rather, although our outer self is wasting away, our inner self is being renewed day by day. [17]For this momentary light affliction is producing for us an eternal weight of glory beyond all comparison, [18]as we look not to what is seen but to what is unseen; for what is seen is transitory, but what is unseen is eternal.

In this final section of our Pauline text, Paul communicates his understanding of how the present and future interact in our lives with several more opposites:

| | |
|---|---|
| Outer self | Inner self |
| Wasting away | Renewed day by day |
| Momentary light affliction | Eternal weight of glory |
| Seen | Unseen |
| Transitory | Eternal |

Paul is telling us that we have one foot in the present and the other in eternity. Right now, we may experience our outer self—those earthen vessels—as "wasting away," whether through illness, age, fatigue, or stress. We experience "affliction." We experience what can be seen. But this is all transitory. In the meantime, our inner self is being "renewed" by our unity with Christ—strengthened, refreshed, restored. No matter what the outer self experiences, the inner self can always experience newness and growth! We are being prepared for an "eternal weight

What are some ways that you experience your outer self changing? What about your inner self? How are the outer self and the inner self connected?

of glory"—that which is unseen, that which is eternal.

St. Paul has a way of putting things in perspective. Our anxieties and worries, the stress we carry with us, are real, but they do not control us. If, like Paul, we are "in Christ," then we cannot be "driven to despair" (v. 8). Rather, we are being renewed by the dying, by the life, of Jesus.

Does Paul's "reframing" of human suffering as a sharing in the death and life of Jesus resonate with you? Why or why not?

## *Praying the Word / Sacred Reading*

### *A Prayer in Times of Stress*

Lord God, you have promised
that you are never far away,
  even when I feel alone;
that you will never leave me,
  even when I feel abandoned;
that I will never be overcome,
  even when I feel defeated;
that there is beauty where I do not see it;
that there is music where I do not hear it;
that there is life where I do not feel it.

Whatever I am going through,
whatever the future may bring,
whatever questions I have,
whatever bad news I hear,
whatever pain comes my way,
whatever I cannot control,
be with me, my God, and this will be enough.

Whatever I lose,
whatever I have lost,

whatever is said,
whatever is done,
whatever is broken,
whatever won't heal,
be with me, my God, and this will be enough.

Whatever decisions I struggle to make,
whatever pressure weighs down on me,
whatever I regret,
whatever I confess,
whatever I remember,
whatever I forget,
be with me, my God, and this will be enough.

Fill my restless spirit with your presence,
   and this will be enough.
Fill my tired mind with your peace,
   and this will be enough.
Fill my aching heart with your love,
   and this will be enough.
Amen.

## Living the Word

*Paul's understanding of the coexistence of death and life is a source of great hope for Christians who are living through stressful times. Here are a few ways to cultivate hope in your life. If you are in a group setting, share with one another some of your own ideas for growing in hope.*

- *Keep a prayer journal. Write down your worries, and "cast your burden on the Lord"*

(Ps 55:22, NRSV). *After you have written what is in your heart, read back over what you have written. Then spend a few moments listening with the ears of your heart. How is God responding to you?*

- **Instead of doing something, undo something.** *Can you identify a negative influence in your life that brings you down and adds to your anxiety? Sometimes a simple change in our lives such as watching less upsetting news coverage or spending less time alone can improve our outlook and help us feel more hopeful. Try to identify a negative influence or habit and eliminate it from your daily routine.*

- **Get in touch with nature.** *Remember how Jesus said that we should look to the birds and the flowers as examples of living without worry? Nature also offers us many inspiring lessons about the fruitful, natural relationship between death and life (e.g., the dead leaves of fall break down to fertilize the earth for the new growth of spring). Spend some time outdoors and draw hope from the beauty, the natural cycles, and the life all around you.*

# Put on Love

*Begin in quiet, asking God to assist you in your prayer and study. Then read the passage from Colossians about how we live in the peace of Christ.*

Colossians 3:12-17

¹²Put on then, as God's chosen ones, holy and beloved, heartfelt compassion, kindness, humility, gentleness, and patience, ¹³bearing with one another and forgiving one another, if one has a grievance against another; as the Lord has forgiven you, so must you also do. ¹⁴And over all these put on love, that is, the bond of perfection. ¹⁵And let the peace of Christ control your hearts, the peace into which you were also called in one body. And be thankful. ¹⁶Let the word of Christ dwell in you richly, as in all wisdom you teach and admonish one another, singing psalms, hymns, and spiritual songs with gratitude in your hearts to God. ¹⁷And whatever you do, in word or in deed,

do everything in the name of the Lord Jesus, giving thanks to God the Father through him.

> *Following a few moments of quiet reflection on the passage from Paul to the Colossians, consider the information provided in Setting the Scene. Continue using the occasional questions in the margins for personal reflection or for group discussion.*

## Setting the Scene

In our final passage, we turn to another text attributed to Paul. This passage will introduce us to a classic Pauline theme: *Christians have been transformed in Christ, and they should act accordingly.* Elsewhere, Paul summarizes the idea by saying: "[T]he only thing that counts is faith working through love" (Gal 5:6, NRSV). For Paul, it is never enough to simply say one is a Christian or to believe the "right things." Rather, being "in Christ" is an experience that transforms the human person from the inside out, from the top to the bottom, from now into eternity. This transformation is a dynamic reality—the transformed Christian lives and breathes Christ. The transformed Christian lives and breathes *love*.

This concept is entirely relevant to our discussion of finding peace in a stressful world. The single most powerful antidote to stress is love—both giving and receiving love. In this passage from Colossians, Paul will emphasize both. As baptized Christians we are part of a transformed community (albeit one that does not always

exhibit the love that transforms it!). "Belonging" bestows on us the gift of this community that is being transformed by love, and it simultaneously places on us the responsibility of loving others. Paul seems to be saying that we were made for this—that all the qualities he encourages us to embrace—kindness, compassion, humility, gentleness, patience, forgiveness, thankfulness, love—are the things that will bring us the true peace of Christ. Miraculously, when our focus turns to others rather than ourselves, we become happier and more at peace. This mixture of theological insight, spiritual coaxing, and old-fashioned common sense is typically Pauline and remains effective in guiding even the modern reader toward a life of real peace.

The Christian community at Colossae, like all of Paul's communities, faced challenges and uncertainties. Other teachers often came into the communities Paul founded and taught them ideas and beliefs that conflicted with Paul's teachings. The Colossians were apparently being taught to adopt certain rigid practices and beliefs. In this letter, Paul is encouraging the community to hold fast to his message about the power of Christ and the essence of Christian faith. Paul insists that the Christian life does not consist in rigidity but rather in an authentic life of love.

*Colossians 3:12-17 will be explored a few verses at a time to deepen your understanding and appreciation.*

## Understanding the Scene Itself

<sup>12</sup>**Put on then, as God's chosen ones, holy and beloved, heartfelt compassion, kindness, humility, gentleness, and patience, <sup>13</sup>bearing with one another and forgiving one another, if one has a grievance against another; as the Lord has forgiven you, so must you also do.**

Immediately prior to this passage, Paul has been writing to the Colossians about baptism. He uses metaphorical language that recalls the baptismal garment worn by the newly baptized to symbolize their new life in Christ (e.g., 3:10: "put on the new self"). Paul continues using that language here, reminding the Colossians that putting on an outer garment is not enough—they must also "put on" distinctively Christlike virtues: compassion that comes from deep within ("heartfelt" here literally means "from the gut"), kindness, humility, gentleness, patience, and forgiveness.

Note how Paul addresses his community as "God's chosen ones, holy and beloved." These affectionate words have several effects. First, they remind the Colossians of their dignity before God. They are set aside and loved by God. Second, the address serves as a clear reminder of God's expectations for his beloved ones. The Colossians (and the whole body of Christ) are

> Humility has a quiet, liberating power that releases us from the sense of competition so common in relationships and communities. Who has served as an example of humility in your life? How do you incorporate what you have learned from him or her into your own life?

Recall a time when forgiving someone or being forgiven by someone brought you peace. What have your own life experiences taught you about forgiveness?

holy, set apart, chosen for a special purpose. As Paul continues, we are reminded that this purpose, this calling, is characterized by virtues such as compassion and gentleness.

These initial verses orient us toward the peaceful, life-giving effects of living in Christ, which really means living *like* Christ. In particular, Paul singles out forgiveness as something we do in imitation of Christ ("the Lord") who has forgiven each of us.

**14And over all these put on love, that is, the bond of perfection.**

Paul continues utilizing the language of the baptismal garment: "over all these put on love." (The New Jerusalem Bible offers an even more literal translation: "*Over all these clothes*, put on love.") Once one has dressed in the Christlike qualities of kindness, compassion, and forgiveness, there is still one more item of "clothing" to put on—love.

Do you ever expect "perfection" from yourself in the modern sense of "no mistakes"? How does this expectation contribute to your stress? When have you experienced "perfection" in the biblical sense of wholeness, completion, and harmony?

What does Paul mean by "the bond of perfection"? As modern readers, we tend to think of perfection as "no mistakes" or "nothing out of order." But for the ancients, perfection meant completion, wholeness, and harmony. It was a beauty that was experienced rather than a quality that could be measured.

Understood in this way, love is not a perfection sought for the benefit of one person. It is for the benefit of the entire community—for the sake of its wholeness and harmony. As Paul explains in 1 Corinthians 8:1: "love builds up."

Love is the primary envoy of peace in any community. As love promotes harmony, it "builds up" and brings about a sense of wholeness, not only in individuals but in communities.

We should note that this is certainly not the only reference in Paul's letters to the primacy of love. Consider these other examples that speak to love's central role in Christian life and in the Christian community:

> "The commandments . . . are summed up in this saying, [namely] 'You shall love your neighbor as yourself.' Love does no evil to the neighbor; hence, love is the fulfillment of the law" (Rom 13:9-10).

> "So faith, hope, love remain, these three; but the greatest of these is love" (1 Cor 13:13).

> "Your every act should be done with love" (1 Cor 16:14).

**¹⁵And let the peace of Christ control your hearts, the peace into which you were also called in one body. And be thankful.**

As Paul continues to instruct the Colossians, he urges them to "let the peace of Christ control [their] hearts." The Greek word translated as "control" here literally means "be the arbiter" or "be the umpire." The peace of Christ—which flows naturally from a life of kindness, compassion,

Why is love the most important quality a Christian can "put on"? What experiences have demonstrated this to you?

What is the "referee" or the "umpire" of your life? In other words, what seems to be controlling your life?

gentleness, patience, forgiveness, and especially love—can literally "referee" our hearts! Rather than being "refereed" by our schedules, our to-do lists, our worries and doubts, or our material things, we can allow the peace of Christ to guide us, to direct our hearts, the very center of our beings.

These encouraging words from Paul continue with a reminder that this "peace of Christ" is not only for our own benefit, but for the benefit of the "one body," the church. This is a theological statement, but it is also a *logical* statement: when we are at peace, we bring peace to whatever community we are connected with—our families, our parishes, our workplaces. Of course, here Paul is speaking specifically of the church—the primary community of the Christian.

Does gratitude come naturally to you, or is it a struggle? How does authentic gratitude change your priorities and bring peace into your life?

Paul then encourages his readers to "be thankful" (*eucharistos*). There is a natural relationship between gratitude and peace. A thankful approach to life creates contentment and stability, qualities that bring us a deep joy that cannot be shaken.

**¹⁶Let the word of Christ dwell in you richly, as in all wisdom you teach and admonish one another, singing psalms, hymns, and spiritual songs with gratitude in your hearts to God.**

This verse gives us a peek into a bit of the early church's liturgical life. The Gospel—or the Good News of Jesus—is to be the central "word" in the life of every Christian. In addition, the psalms and various hymns (including the "Christ hymn" of Colossians 1:15-20) are not only part of the church's prayer, but are considered instructive (used to "teach and admonish"). Another reference to gratitude reminds us of its central importance.

**¹⁷And whatever you do, in word or in deed, do everything in the name of the Lord Jesus, giving thanks to God the Father through him.**

Our final verse provides a beautiful summary of all we have considered together: *"And whatever you do, in word or in deed . . . ."* Paul is offering guidance for our entire lives. He does so with two brief instructions:

*"[D]o everything in the name of the Lord Jesus."* To do something "in the name of" Jesus is to do it as his representative, to do it as though Jesus himself is acting or speaking. This could be seen as a daunting responsibility for the baptized Christian. Or it could be seen as Paul saw it—as the greatest honor and joy of the Christian life. In Galatians 2:20, Paul writes about his own experience of living this way: "I live, no longer I, but Christ lives in me." In other words, we need not strive and strain to be "like Jesus." Instead, we need only let Christ live in us—in his death and in the new life of his resurrection—so that it is no longer we who are in control, but Christ who guides us in "everything."

*"[G]iving thanks to God the Father through [Jesus]."* The thankfulness that Paul has urged us toward is a hallmark of Christian life. Gratitude is a sign of trust. It is the attitude of one who acknowledges God's love and providence, who

What advice from this excerpt of Paul's letter to the Colossians do you find most helpful for finding peace? How can you incorporate this message into your daily life?

believes God will care for us, who no longer needs to worry about the past, present, or future. And so we come full circle to the words of Jesus with which we began: "Do not be afraid any longer, little flock, for your Father is pleased to give you the kingdom" (Luke 12:32). We do not need to be afraid any longer. God has assured us of his loving care. He has given us a share in the life, death, and resurrection of his Son. And we are free to live like Christ in kindness and love, with his peace as the gentle arbiter of our hearts.

### Praying the Word / Sacred Reading

*Reflect for several minutes on how your life is ordered when the peace of Christ is "the arbiter" or "umpire" of your heart. What kinds of things do you do when you are living "in Christ"? How do you treat others? What kinds of things do you think about?*

*Prayerfully read the following passage from Paul's letter to the Philippians. Rest in Christ, pondering with him the things that are true, honorable, just, pure, lovely, and gracious.*

Rejoice in the Lord always. I shall say it again: rejoice! Your kindness should be known to all. The Lord is near. Have no anxiety at all, but in everything, by prayer and petition, with thanksgiving, make your requests known to God. Then the peace of God that surpasses all understanding will guard your hearts and minds in Christ Jesus.

Finally, brothers, whatever is true, whatever is honorable, whatever is just, whatever is pure, whatever is lovely, whatever is gracious, if there is any excellence and if there is anything worthy of praise, think about these things. Keep on doing what you have learned and received and heard and seen in me. Then the God of peace will be with you. (Philippians 4:4-9)

## Living the Word

*An ancient story about the apostle John tells how, as an old man, he would say the same thing over and over to his community: "Little children, love one another." When asked by his (somewhat annoyed) companions why he repeated it so often, he responded, "Because it is the Lord's command, and it is all that is necessary."*

*These words resonate deeply with Paul's message. Love is the primary sign of being one with Christ. And if we are one with Christ, all is well.*

*Embrace John's words, which echo the words of Jesus himself (John 15:17). Repeat them in your own heart—the center of your being—as many times as you can throughout the day. Let this simple love command be the "arbiter" or the "umpire" of your life, the road map of how you will live, the way of life that sets you free from worry and stress, the guiding light that brings you a deep peace that passes all understanding.*

"[P]ut on love. . . . And let the peace of Christ control your hearts" (Col 3:14-15).